Table Of Contents

Illustrations & Charts

Illustrations

Charts

The Basics of
Craps

J. Edward Allen

The Basics of Gambling Series
published by
Gambling Research Institute

First Printing	*October 1984*
Second Printing	*February 1985*
Third Printing	*June 1986*
Fourth Printing	*September 1987*

Copyright ©1984 by Gambling Research Institute

ISBN: 0-9607618-3-7

Book Design and Production—Santa Cruz Typesetting

GRI/Cardoza Publishing
P.O. Box 1500, Cooper Station
New York, NY 10276

I. Introduction

Craps is certainly the most exciting and the fastest of all casino games. There is action, if the player wishes, on every roll of the dice. It's also a game in which one can let loose; it doesn't matter how excited you get at the table, or how you show your emotions. This not only makes the game exciting, but fun as well. However, it's a casino game, after all, and money can be won or lost while playing it. This book will show you how to play the game correctly, how to make the best bets and how to come out a winner if lady luck is on your side.

Each aspect of the game is gone into, so that even the novice, or person unfamiliar with craps will know all that is necessary to play the game intelligently and avoid the worst bets, the ones that favor the house with too much of an edge.

So, good luck. Following the advice outlined in this book will give you the best chance of winning at this most exciting of games.

II. Understanding the Dice

The game of casino craps is played with two dice and each die has six numbered sides.

The numbers are in the form of dots, running from one to six. Thus, with two dice in play, the lowest number that can be rolled is 2; made up of the one spot coming up on each die. The highest number is 12, which is made up of six spots coming up on each die. With two dice in operation, there are thirty-six possible combinations that can be rolled, with the numbers from two to twelve as possibilities.

Casino dice are built to exacting standards, so that there is little chance of certain numbers showing up more often than others because of faulty design or manufacture. They're approximately 3/4 of an inch measured on each side, and are made as close to exact cubes as modern machinery will allow.

When you're playing the game, and it's your turn to roll the dice, if you look closely, you'll see imprinted on the dice two other things besides the dots representing the numbers. First of all, the name of the casino, or its logo will be shown. Secondly, there'll be a code number. Individual sets of dice are made for particular casinos, often coming in a particular color, such as green or red, the most common in American gambling casinos. In addition, code numbers are put on the dice so that cheats can't substitute other dice for the ones regularly used. This safeguards both the casino and the players in the course of a game.

Dice Combinations

The next table shows all the possible combinations of two rolled dice.

The above table is symmetrical in size, with the 7 standing firmly in the center and all other numbers sliding away from it. The 7 can be rolled no matter what number shows up on one die; it is unique in that aspect. For example, a 6 cannot be rolled if a six shows on one die, and an 8 can't be rolled if a 1 shows up on any die.

The seven is the most important number by far in the game of casino craps, and determines all the odds.

Chart 1
Dice Combinations

Number	Combinations	Ways to Roll
2	1-1	One
3	1-2, 2-1	Two
4	1-3, 3-1, 2-2	Three
5	1-4, 4-1, 2-3, 3-2	Four
6	1-5, 5-1, 2-4, 4-2, 3-3	Five
7	1-6, 6-1, 2-5, 5-2, 3-4, 4-3	Six
8	2-6, 6-2, 3-5, 5-3, 4-4	Five
9	3-6, 6-3, 4-5, 5-4	Four
10	4-6, 6-4, 5-5	Three
11	5-6, 6-5	Two
12	6-6	One

Correct Odds, House Payoff and Edge

The **house advantage** or **edge** is the difference between the player's chances of winning the bet, called the **correct odds**, and the casino's actual payoff, called the **house payoff** or simply, the **payoff**. For example, the correct odds of rolling a 7 are 5 to 1. Since the house will payoff only 4 to 1 should the 7 be thrown, they maintain an edge of 16.67 percent on this wager.

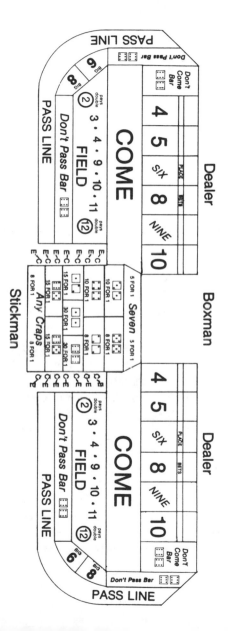

Nevada Craps Layout

III. The Table and Layout

The Table

The average craps table is about the size of a large billiards table and is built to accomodate anywhere from twelve to twenty-four players. There is a felt covered surface known as the **layout**, around which are walls which form the table, and on which are rails to hold the players' chips.

The main purpose of the layout is to give the players what they're at the casino for, action. They have a chance to make a variety of bets, all of which are favorable to the house, that is, the odds on each bet favor the house.

We can see that there are essentially three sections on the layout. There are two identical side areas separated by a center area. The center area is where all the center, or proposition bets are made. As we shall see, none of the bets in this section are worth a red penny; they're all bad, that is, highly unfavorable to the player. The following is the center layout.

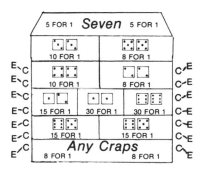

The two side areas are identical and they contain the best wagers for the player to make, since they give the house the smallest advantage over the gamblers. This is the best area to put your money.

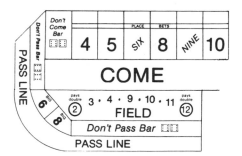

IV. Casino Personnel

The Crew of Dealers

A casino craps crew is made up of four individuals, but only three work the table at one time, with the fourth **on break**, that is, taking a rest from his chores. The crew usually is made up of men, though more and more women are seen as integral parts of craps crews.

The men and women who make up the working crew do not have set jobs at the table. They move around from position to position. This rotation keeps them alert and adds flavor to the game, for each dealer has a different personality and an upbeat dealer or crew can make a game come alive.

The Stickman

One of the dealers faces the other two. He or she is known as the **stickman**, or is said to be **on the stick.**

This is because he or she holds a malleable stick in his hand, which is used first of all, to push the dice to a new shooter, then to gather in dice that have been thrown and to hold them with the stick till all payoffs and collections have been made by the other dealers.

The stickman also is in charge of all the center or **proposition** bets, which are under his direct control. He collects losing bets and pushes them to the boxman, whom we will discuss later. The stickman directs the other dealers to pay off winning bets that occur on the center of the table.

If a player makes a propostion or center bet, the chips are thrown to the stickman to be put in the correct betting box. But the stickman doesn't pay off bets, and has no direct contact with the players except for pushing the dice toward the shooter with his stick.

The dealer on the stick has one other important duty. He calls the game. If a new shooter is to be selected, he announces *"new shooter coming out."* If there is a come-out roll, he announces that as well. After the dice are thrown, he calls the number thrown, such as *"five"*. He may also add, *"five, no field,"* to indicate that it is not paid off on the field bets.

Often the personality of the stickman infuses the craps game and determines whether it will be lively or dull.

Dealers On-Base

These are the two standing dealers who face the stickman, and each covers an end area of the layout. They have direct contact with the players. They make change, **change color** (change chips for others of different denominations), pay off winning bets and collect losing ones.

They also handle the players' chips when they want to make center bets or bets they can't reach, such as odds bets on don't come and come points.

These dealers are said to be **on base**. When you first come to a table, it will be a dealer on base that you'll give your cash to. He'll give you the correct casino chips as soon as the sum is verified by the boxman.

The standing dealer will also answer any questions you might have as to the table limits, how much you can wager on any particular bet and whether or not single or double odds are permitted at the table.

Each standing dealer has a **marker puck,** a black and white round plastic disk, which is on the black side in the corner don't come box prior to a come-out roll. This disk is turned up to its white side and put into a point number box after a point is established on the *"come-out roll"*. A come-out roll will be explained later.

First and foremost, the dealer is there to help you, the player, to make certain your bets have been correctly made and to answer any of your questions about the game.

The Boxman

The crew of dealers wear the house uniform, but the boxman is usually dressed in a jacket or suit. He is in charge of the game, and sits between the two on-base dealers, facing the stickman.

The boxman supervises the game, makes sure that the payoffs are correct, makes certain that the cash given to the dealer is verified, and in short, he sits there protecting the casino's bankroll, for most of the chips on the table are right in front of him, under his domain and protection.

If the dice are thrown off the table, they must first be returned to the boxman, who examines the die or dice to make sure they haven't been tampered with and are the same die or dice that were thrown, and not new dice inserted in the game by cheats. To do this, he looks for both the casino logo and the coded number on all casino dice.

If there's a dispute between a player and a dealer, as sometimes happens, the boxman has the final word. Generally, he will side with the player, unless it is a flagrant objection by the player, but thereafter, in further disputes, he'll not give the player the benefit of the doubt.

Casino Executives

Since craps table revenue is an important aspect of the profits of a casino, not only are the crew of dealers and boxman involved with the game, but behind the table, in the *craps pit* are several other casino employees, executives of the house. These might include a **floorman**, who supervises a couple of tables, and is there in case any of the players want to get credit. And above him, in charge of all the craps tables in what is known as the craps pit, is the **pitboss**, the final authority on credit and disputes.

Tipping

Tipping, or **toking** as it is called in the casinos, is a voluntary practice. Only the crew of dealers are tipped, not the boxman or the casino executives. If a player is winning a lot and feels in a buoyant mood, or he has received good services from the dealers, then he may tip them. The usual practice is to make a bet for *the boys* by throwing a chip toward the center or proposition bets, and making one of those high yielding but poor odds bets. Just say *"for the boys"*. The crew will understand that this bet is for them, and should thank you for it. They appreciate tokes because that's the main source of their income.

V. How to Play Craps

In this section we're going to study just how to play craps, and show the essential game, what's involved and so forth. So let's imagine that we know nothing about the game, and we're in a gambling casino, approaching a craps table. There are a few open spots around the rails and we move into one of them.

The first thing we want to do is make a bet; but before we can do that, we should change our cash into casino chips, or **checks** as the professionals call them. We can play with cash, make bets in cash all night long, but the casino discourages this, for it's cumbersome and slows the game down, and has to be counted and recounted. Chips are easier, fit into betting areas better, and can be paid off more easily. In fact, even if you wager in cash, you'll be paid off with chips.

Casino Chips

Chips usually come in standard denominations of $1, $5, $25 and $100. Some casinos have $500 or larger denomination chips and others have smaller denominations, down to 25¢ chips. But for purposes of this book we're going to stick with the $1 to $100 chips.

All right, we're at the table, and we take some cash out of our pocket. We're going to gamble with $200 worth. This cash is given to the standing dealer nearest us, and the cash will go over to the seated boxman who'll count and verify its amount. Once it's verified, he'll tell the dealer to give you $200 in chips, while the cash is pushed down with a paddle into a slot on the table, to fall into a **drop box.**

Now the casino has our cash, but we have its chips. The dealer will ask what denominations we want. We might ask for a stack of twenty $5 chips and four $25 chips. Long-time gamblers refer to $5 chips as **nickels** and $25 chips as **quarters.** The dealer will hand you twenty $5 chips and four $25 chips and now you're ready to make a bet.

The Shooter

When you arrive at the table, someone will be ready to throw the dice. This is the **shooter.** Whatever he throws is what determines whether bets are won or lost.

Let's assume that a new shooter is about to be given the dice. Each player gets a turn at being a shooter. The dice go around the table in a clockwise manner. Anyone who's selected as the shooter may pass up the chance; there's no stigma attached to not being a shooter. If the dice are refused, then the next person, to that player's left, will be offered the dice.

The shooter will be given from six to eight dice, of which he'll select only two. He will generally roll with these same dice for his entire shoot; through sometimes eccentric players will change the dice or if one is rolled off the table or temporarily lost, another one will replace the lost die.

But this decision rests solely with the shooter. Other players at the table can't demand that the dice be changed. While a person is a shooter, he or she is the center of attention.

VI. The Line and Free-Odds Bets

Making A Bet

Before the shooter rolls the dice for the first time, or after he has made his point (which will be explained later) there is a *come-out* roll. Prior to the come-out roll, most of the players at the table bet either for or against the dice by making either a pass-line or don't pass bet. This is done by putting a chip or chips into the appropriate areas on the layout. By far the most popular bet in casino craps is the pass-line wager.

Pass-Line Wager and Come-Out Roll

The area that accomodates the pass-line bet runs the full length of each side area, to give the bettors easy access to this wager.

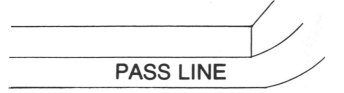

PASS LINE

This bet can only be made prior to the opening roll of the dice, the come-out roll. A come-out roll can easily be ascertained, for there is a round disk that is black and white and when it is resting on its black side in the corner of the numbered boxes, in the don't come box, then there is a come-out roll about to commence.

When this same disk is on its white side and in one of the numbered boxes on the layout, in the 4, 5, 6, 8, 9 or 10 box, then that is the point established by the come-out roll, and no more line bets are permitted. A **line bet** is either a pass-line or don't pass wager.

The come-out roll is the most important throw in craps. It determines either immediate wins or losses, or what point is established.

The bettor wagering on the pass-line wants the dice to win, or pass. He is known as the **right** bettor, and wins immediately at even-money if:

A 7 or 11 is rolled on the come-out.

He loses immediately if:

A 2, 3 or 12, all known as **craps** is rolled on the come-out.

When a shooter rolls a 2, 3 or 12, he is said to have

crapped out, but he doesn't lose his shoot. After all pass-line bets are collected, and all don't pass bets paid off, he continues his shoot.

If the come-out roll is a 4, 5, 6, 8, 9 or 10, that number is the **point**, and must be repeated before a 7 is thrown for the pass-line bet to win. All other numbers are immaterial to this result, once a point has been established on the come-out. For example, if the point is 4, and subsequently an 11, 12, 3, 2, 8, 8, 9 and 4 is rolled, the pass-line bet is won, because the 4 repeated before a 7 was thrown. None of the other numbers rolled mattered as to this result.

Don't Pass Bet

A player betting **don't pass** is betting against the dice, wagering that they don't pass, or win. He is known as a **wrong** bettor, and he places his chip or chips in the smaller area reserved for don't pass.

A don't pass bettor wins immediately at even-money if:
A 2 or 3 is rolled on the come-out.

He loses immediately if:
A 7 or 11 is rolled.

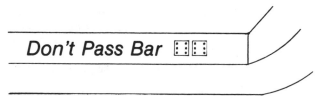

22

If a 12 is rolled, there's a standoff, and he neither wins nor loses. In some gambling jurisdictions the 2 is substituted for the 12, with the same effect. The 12 or 2 is **barred**, permitting the casino to keep its edge on don't pass wagers.

If a point number is established, the don't pass bettor wins if a 7 comes up before the point is repeated. He'll lose if the point is repeated before a seven comes up again. The house edge on all line bets, whether they be pass-line or don't pass, is 1.4%. When a player makes these bets, he is giving the house or casino a theoretical win expectation of $1.40 for each $100 bet. However, he can reduce this house edge substantially by making another bet at the same time he makes the line bet. This additional wager is not shown on the layout, but is permissable, and all intelligent craps players should make it. It's known as the **free-odds** bet.

The Free-Odds Bet

This bet can only be made *after* a point number has been established on the come-out. It's made by putting additional chips behind the original bet for pass-line bettors. If won, this additional wager will be paid off at true and correct odds, giving the casino no advantage whatsoever on the wager. That's why it's known as a free-odds bet. If the point is a 4 or 10, the free-odds bet will be paid off at 2-1; a 5 or 9 will be paid off at 3-2, and a 6 or 8 will be paid off at 6-5.

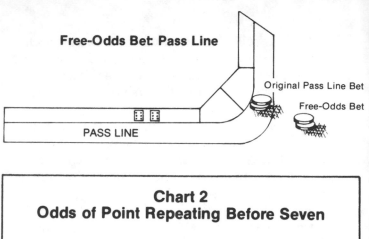

Free-Odds Bet: Pass Line

Original Pass Line Bet

Free-Odds Bet

PASS LINE

Chart 2
Odds of Point Repeating Before Seven

Point Number	Correct Odds	House Payoff
4 or 10	2 to 1	2 to 1
5 or 9	3 to 2	3 to 2
6 or 8	6 to 5	6 to 5

In most casinos the player is limited to a free-odds bet equal to his original pass-line bet. In those casinos the bet is then called a **single odds** bet. But the good news is that, even if one is limited to single odds, a bettor can wager a little more behind the line in certain instances.

For example, if a player bet $5 on the pass-line and the point is 5 or 9, then he's permitted to wager $6 as a free odds bet because the payoff is 3-2, and most casinos won't pay off in half-dollar increments.

When the point is 4 or 10, no matter what is bet the same amount must be wagered as a free odds bet since the payoff is 2-1.

But if the point is 6 and 8, most casinos will permit a $5 free odds bet if the player bets at least $3 on the pass-line. Unless $5 is bet behind the line the payoff on the odds bet won't be the correct 6-5, because the house doesn't pay off in half-dollars. For example, if a gambler bet $6 on the pass-line, and then $6 on the free odds bet if the point was 8, the free odds payoff would be $7, which represents $6 for the first $5 bet, and only $1 at even-money for the extra dollar bet. In order to get the correct free odds return, when the point is 6 or 8, the bets behind the line must be in increments of $5. And when the point is 5 or 9, then the free odds bet must be in increments of $2.

What happens when a pass-line bet and free-odds bet win? What's the payoff? Let's assume a player bets $10 on the pass-line and a point is established. He or she then puts $10 behind the line as a free-odds bet. Here are the payoffs:

Chart 3
Single Odds Payoffs: Right Bettors

Point	Pass-Line Payoff	Free-Odds Payoff	Total
4 or 10	$10	$20 (2-1)	$30
5 or 9	$10	$15 (3-2)	$25
6 or 8	$10	$12 (6-5)	$22

If the 7 comes up before the point is repeated, then the player loses both the pass-line and free odds bets.

25

When making a free-odds bet, the player reduces the overall house edge from 1.4% to 0.8%, a substantial reduction.

In some casinos, players are permitted to make **double odds** bets. In these casinos, the bettor can place *twice his original bet* behind the line as a free-odds bet. Thus, if he bet $10 on the pass-line, he can put $20 behind the line at correct payoffs. Here's what these payoffs would look like with a $10 pass-line and $20 free odds bet.

Chart 4
Double Odds Payoffs: Right Bettors

Point Payoff	Pass-Line Payoff	Free-Odds Payoff	Total Payoff
4 or 10	$10	$40 (2-1)	$50
5 or 9	$10	$30 (3-2)	$40
6 or 8	$10	$24 (6-5)	$34

A double free-odds bet reduces the house edge down to 0.6%.

Free-odds wagers can be made at any time after a point is established, and can be removed at the player's option at any time prior to a seven-out or the point being repeated. But since it's to the advantage of a player to make a free-odds bet, he or she should always make it, and it should never be removed.

Don't Pass—Laying Free-Odds

A gambler who bets don't pass, betting that the dice will not pass, that the 7 will come up before the point is repeated, can also make free-odds bets. But whereas the pass-line bettor is taking odds, the don't pass bettor is **laying odds**. By making this advantageous bet, the player reduces the casino's overall edge from 1.4% to 0.8%.

Free-Odds Bet: Don't Pass

free-odds bet

original don't pass bet

Don't Pass Bar

Chart 5
Odds of Rolling Seven Before Point Repeats

Point Number	Correct Odds	House Payoff
4 or 10	1 to 2	1 to 2
5 or 9	2 to 3	2 to 3
6 or 8	5 to 6	5 to 6

For example, if a don't pass bettor had put down $10 in the don't pass area and the come-out roll was a 5, then 5 is the point. Now this same don't pass gambler can bet $15 as a free odds bet. What he is doing is betting $15 to win $10, since he is laying 3-2 against the 5 being made. Should the shooter seven-out and not repeat the point, then the don't pass player would win $10 for his don't pass bet and an additional $10 for his free odds bet.

When single odds are permitted, they are determined by the *payoff* amount, not the amount that can be laid against the point. Thus, if the line bet is $10 and the point is 4 or 10, a $20 free odds bet laid against these points will yield a payoff of $10. Likewise $15 against a 5 or 9 will give a payoff of $10, and with a 6 or 8 as a point, the payoff will be $10 if $12 is laid against these points. The following table will show the payoffs if $10 is bet on don't pass and single odds are laid against the various points.

Chart 6
Single Odds Payoffs: Wrong Bettors

Point	Don't Pass Payoff	Free-Odds Payoff	Total Payoff
4 or 10	$10	$10 ($20-$10)	$20
5 or 9	$10	$10 ($15-$10)	$20
6 or 8	$10	$10 ($12-$10)	$20

Like other free-odds bets, these may be laid or taken off at any time after a point is established, at the option of the player.

Some casinos allow double odds bets, and in those houses, a player may lay double the amount he can in a single odds casino. Again, the payoff, not the amount of the odds bet determines how much may be laid.

Thus, a gambler betting $10 as a don't pass bet can lay $40 ($40-$20) if the point is 4 or 10, $30 ($30-$20) if the point is 5 or 9, and $24 ($24-$20) if the point is 6 or 8.

When double odds are laid, the house edge is reduced to 0.6%.

Of course, if the point is made, the don't pass player loses both his original don't pass bet and the double odds free bet.

VII. Come and Don't Come Bets

These bets are a little difficult for most players to figure out, but in essence, they're really not hard to understand. And they offer the best odds on the table, along with the line bets, so a craps player should be conversant with them and use them to advantage.

Come Bets

A large section of the layout is devoted to come bets.

COME

This bet is the same as a pass-line bet, except that it can only be made *after* the come-out roll. That's the only difference, really. Let's assume that on the come-out roll, the number thrown was a 9. That's the point. Now, any player can make a come bet.

The come bet is made by putting a chip or chips into the come box. On the very next roll of the dice, if the number is 7 or 11, the come bet wins at even-money. If it's a 2, 3 or 12, the come bet loses immediately. If any other number is rolled, a 4, 5, 6, 8, 9 or 10, then that's the come point. The chips are moved by the dealer to the appropriate number box, which also house the place bets (discussed later).

The player may make a free-odds bet on the come point just as he could on the pass-line point. If its single odds, then a bet equal to the come bet will be given to the dealer and the dealer should be told "odds". He'll place the chip or chips at a slight tilt on the come bet in the appropriate box number. If it's double odds at this casino then a bet double the original come bet can be handed to the dealer as an odds bet.

Let's assume, after the come-out roll of 9, that the next number is 10, and a player had bet $5 on the come. This $5 is moved to box 10, and the player gives the dealer an additional $5 as a free-odds bet. Now, as to the come bet, all that he's concerned with is whether a 10 repeats before the 7. All other numbers are immaterial to the outcome of this bet. If a 10 repeats, the player will be paid $5 for the come bet, and $10 for the free-odds bet at 2-1.

If a 7 comes up before the 10 repeats, then the

player loses both the come and free-odds bets.

Let's assume that instead of a 10 being thrown on the first roll after the come-out, a 7 was rolled. This is an immediate winner for the come bet even though it loses the pass-line bet. Each come roll must be treated as a bet separate from a pass-line wager.

Now, after that 7 is rolled, a player can't make another come bet because there's a new come-out roll, and come bets can only be made after a come-out roll, not at the same time.

The only difference other than timing between a pass-line and come bet is that, if a 7 is thrown on the come-out roll and the player has one or more come bets working, he loses the underlying come bets (because a 7 came up before these number were repeated) but doesn't lose the free-odds bets.

On the come-out roll, the free-odds bets on come wagers aren't *working*. That is, they're **off**. Thus if a player had come bets of $10 each on the 5 and 6, for instance, and also had $10 free-odds on each of those come points, and a 7 is rolled on the come-out roll, he'd lose only $20 on the underlying bets and the $20 in free-odds bets would be returned to him.

Conversely, if either the 5 or 6 had been thrown on the come-out roll, the player would be paid only $10 for the number repeating, and wouldn't get the additional odds bet as a winner. It would simply be returned to him.

Why make come bets? Well, they give the house the same low percentage that it gets on pass-line bets, and enables the player to make a whole series of consecutive wagers at good odds, so that, if the dice get *hot* and a lot of numbers are rolled before a 7 comes up, he can really make a lot of money in a short period of time. But he must remember that when that 7 shows, all the come bets are lost, erased from the table.

Don't Come Bets

The don't come box is much smaller than the come box on the layout, usually tucked in at the end of the place number boxes.

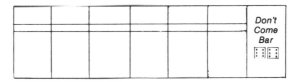

There is usually not that much action on don't come, but that doesn't mean it isn't a valid bet. It's the same as a don't pass bet except for timing, and after the bet is made a player can lay odds against the number just as he or she can on a don't pass bet. The house edge is the same as a don't pass bet, 0.8% when single odds are laid and 0.6% when double odds are laid.

After a come point is rolled, the chip or chips will be taken from the don't come box by the dealer and placed in the area above the numbered box of that come point. Now, the player must give the dealer additional chips to lay odds against the number repeating.

On a don't come bet, if a 7 or 11 is rolled, it's an immediate loser for the don't come player. If a 2 or 3 is rolled, it's an immediate winner at even-money, and if a 12 is rolled, it's a standoff. The same as don't pass in all respects except for timing.

Unlike come bets, don't come bets and odds are always working, even on the come-out roll, so that the player's underlying don't come bet and odds bets are always at risk. On the other hand, if a 7 comes up on the come-out roll, then all the don't come bets are winners, including the free-odds bets laid against the numbers.

Why make don't come bets? The player is hoping for a cold run of dice, where no numbers are repeated. So, after several don't come bets are established, he hopes a 7 comes up and wins all the bets for him. Of course, if a lot of numbers repeat, then he'll be losing those same bets. But the house edge is very small and on a cold table, it's a good way to make money fast.

Free-Odds Bet: Come & Don't Come

Dealer will place free-odds bet atop original bet but offset to distinguish from come or don't come bet.

don't come and free-odds bet

8

NINE

10

come and free-odds bet

34

VIII. Place Numbers and Place Bets

The area where place bets can be made is rather large, for not only do place bets get a lot of action, but the same area holds the come and don't come bets.

		PLACE	BETS		
4	5	SIX	8	NINE	10

Place bets can be made on one or more of the numbers that are point numbers; 4, 5, 6, 8, 9 and 10. A place bet can be made at any time, even prior to a come-out roll, but place bets are off and not working on the come-out roll, unless the player wishes them to be working and so instructs the dealer.

The place bets can be made in any denomination up to the house limit, which is generally $500 on all numbers but the 6 and 8, which have $600 limits. They should be made in increments of $5 for all numbers but the 6 and 8, which are in increments of $6, because of the payoffs. Like come bets, they're favored by players betting *right* or with the dice, and like come bets, they allow action on every roll of the dice. But unlike come bets, a place bet doesn't have to repeat twice to get paid off. Once it's made it gets paid off if that number is rolled.

The gambler, to get this kind of action, pays a price. And the price is the house edge, which is much higher than the casino advantage on come bets.

Chart 7
Odds on Place Numbers

Place Number	Casino Payoff	Correct Odds	Casino Edge
4 and 10	9-5	2-1	6.67%
5 and 9	7-5	3-2	4.0%
6 and 8	7-6	6-5	1.52%

As we can easily see, the only possible worthwhile place bet is on the 6 and 8; otherwise the house edge is just too much.

Not only can place bets be made at any time, but they can be raised, lowered or removed at the player's option at any time, as well. Just hand chips to the dealer or instruct him to remove your chips.

Why make place bets? There's really no reason to do so, unless betting on the 6 and 8. If there's a long hot roll, with many numbers repeating, the payoffs can be tremendous. But the house edge is also horrendous, and will eat up the bankroll before a player reaps the benefit of these long rolls.

Buying the 4 and 10

The house edge on the 4 and 10 can be reduced to 4.73% by **buying** either or both numbers. You make this bet by instructing the dealer that you are *"buying"* the 4 or 10 or both numbers, and then handing him the correct number of chips. A buy button will then be put on those chips. The payoff will be 2-1, but each time you get paid off, you pay the equivalent of a 5% commission. In most casinos this commission must be paid at the time the numbers are bought.

Either buying or placing the 4 and 10 is not recommended because of the large house edge.

Lay Wagers

Players who bet against the dice can **lay** bets against any of the point numbers, by so instructing the dealers that they are *laying* against one or more of these numbers. A 5% commission must be paid at this time. This gives the casino the following edges:

```
┌─────────────────────────────────────────┐
│                Chart 8                   │
│        House Edge on Lay Wager           │
│                                          │
│     Number              Casino Edge      │
│     4 and 10              2.44%          │
│     5 and 9              3.23%           │
│     6 and 8             4.0%            │
│                                          │
└─────────────────────────────────────────┘
```

Like place bets, chips are given to the dealer and these bets can be made at any time, in any combinations, or reduced or taken off at any time.

IX.   Other Bets

Field Bets

These bets are the favorite of beginning or ignorant players, because they're easy to make, can be made at any time on any roll of the dice, and are paid off or lost immediately. But there's a price to pay, and that's a high casino edge.

The Field Bet takes up a prominent place on the casino layout.

```
pays           pays
double  3 · 4 · 9 · 10 · 11  double
 (2)        FIELD            (12)
```

All those numbers look inviting. If a 2 or 12 is thrown, it pays at 2-1. All the other numbers, 3, 4, 9, 10 and 11 pay off at even-money. When the 2 and 12 pay off at 2-1, the house edge on a field bet is 5.5%.

When either the 2 or 12 is paid off at 3-1, then the house edge drops off to 2.70%. This is the case in Atlantic City, Northern Nevada and Downtown Las Vegas. On the Strip, the house edge is 5.5%.

In either case, it's not the best kind of bet to make. The numbers that are missing, the 5, 6, 7 and 8 come up more ways than the numbers on the field bet layout, and though it's a simple bet to make, that's not the reason one should make a field bet.

Why should one make a field bet? There's really no reason to. Avoid it.

Big Six and Big Eight

This bet is prominently displayed, but only small timers make it, putting down a dollar or two and hoping that the 6 or 8 will come up before the 7 is rolled, so that they can collect their even-money winnings.

But there are only five ways to make either a 6 or 8, and six ways to roll a 7, so that the true odds against making the 6 or 8 is 6-5, and when the casino pays off at even-money, it has a 9.09% edge. This bet should never be made except in Atlantic City casinos which will pay off the Big 6 and Big 8 at 7-6, the same as a 6 or 8 place bet, if the bettor puts at least $6 or increments of $6 in the Big 6 or Big 8 box. Otherwise avoid this bet.

Proposition or Center Bets

These bets take up the whole center of the layout and are under the control of the stickman. None of these bets should ever be made, since the house edge is horrendous.

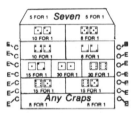

Though the stickman will physically handle the placing and removing of bets in this area, it is with the dealer that the player will generally make his bets and receive his payoffs.

The center bets may be divided into one-roll and other proposition bets.

One Roll Bets

A One-Roll wager wins or loses depending on the very next throw of the dice. The following table shows the true odds against rolling any of these numbers. Since there are thirty-six possible combinations, the odds are figured by dividing the number of ways to roll any particular number into 36.

Chart 9
Odds of One Roll Bets

Number	Ways to Roll	Odds Against On Single Roll
2 or 12	1	35-1
3 or 11	2	17-1
7	6	5-1

Any Seven
Any Seven pays off at 4 to 1, whereas the true odds are 5-1 against a seven being rolled on the next roll, giving the house a 16.67% edge. Sometimes the bet is paid off at 5 for 1, which is the same as 4-1. When you see a "for" between odds numbers, reduce the first number by one. Therefore, 5 for 1 means 4-1.

Any Craps
The true odds against rolling either a 2, 3 or 12 on a single roll is 8-1, but the casino only pays 7-1, giving it an 11.1% edge.

The 2 or 12
If you bet that the next roll of the dice will be a 2, the odds are 35-1 against this happening. The same odds apply to a 12, since there is only one way to make either number. The casino pays only 30-1 on these wagers, giving it an advantage of 13.89%.

The 3 or 11

The true odds against rolling a 3 on the next throw of the dice is 17-1. The same odds apply to the 11, since either can only be made in two ways. The house pays off at only 15-1, giving it an advantage of 11.1%.

Horn Bet

This bet is often seen in Atlantic City or Northern Nevada, and requires 4 chips placed on the 2, 3, 11 and 12, and since the casino pays off at its usual bad odds if any one is rolled, you're getting four bad bets at once. Don't make a horn bet.

Other Proposition Bets

The Hardways

These aren't one-roll bets. When a player bets on a hardway number, he is wagering that the number will come up hard rather than easy, or before a 7 is rolled.

A hardway is the number 4 coming up as 2-2, the 6 coming up as 3-3, the eight coming up as 4-4 and the 10 coming up as 5-5. In other words, with these four numbers, they'll come up hard if identical spots show on each die.

If a 4 is rolled as a 1-3, it's an **easy** number. Remember, the easy ways and the 7 defeat a hardway bet.

Hard 4 and Hard 10

The true odds on these bets are 8-1, but the casino pays off at 7-1, giving it an 11.1% edge. Don't make the bet.

Hard 6 and Hard 8

The true odds on these bets are 10-1, but the casino will only pay 9-1, giving it an edge of 9.09%. This bet should never be made.

X. Winning Craps Play

There are two ways to approach a craps table. One is to bet with the dice, hoping they'll pass, that numbers will repeat, and that the come-out roll will feature a lot of 7s and 11s. A bettor who wants the dice to pass is known as a **right** bettor. There is no moral interpretation of the term. It simply designates a player betting with the dice.

A player who doesn't want the dice to pass, who bets don't pass, is looking for a lot of craps, 2s and 3s on the come-out and a lot of 7s after a point is established. This bettor is wagering against the dice and is known as a **wrong** bettor.

The odds are roughly the same whether you bet right or wrong. You have an equal chance of winning, but remember, casino craps is a negative game, and only luck and correct and smart play will make you a winner. If you make foolish bets, that is, bets in which the house has a big edge over you, there's hardly any chance to walk away a winner from a casino craps table.

Right Bettors—Correct Play

A right player should only make bets which give the house its minimum edge. Therefore, the best and most conservative method of play is to make a pass-line wager, and if a point is established, to take the maximum odds allowed on that point. If uncertain about how much you can wager as an odds bet, ask the dealer.

Then, if the player wants to have a little more action, he can make a come bet or two come bets, also taking the maximum free-odds.

Betting this way, a lucky or hot roll of the dice can win a bit of money, and the player is only giving the house 0.8% in a single odds game and 0.6% in a double odds game.

This kind of gambler will be known as a *tough* player, because he's making only the best bets, and giving the house very little in the way of an edge. If lady luck shines down upon him, he can make a good bit of change with this method.

For the more aggresive bettor, after making a pass-line and one or two come bets, all with maximum free-odds, he can then cover the 6 or 8 if they're not already bet, by making place wagers on these numbers. Here the player will be giving the casino a bigger edge, 1.52%. But if the dice pass and some long rolls develop, the gambler betting this way can make a lot of money.

But don't under any circumstances make any other bet, no matter how tempting the payoffs may be. The house edge is just too great, and will wear down your bankroll in no time flat. Craps is a fast game, and a game in which you can lose your money fast. So be careful and bet smart, in the manner we suggested.

Wrong Bettors—Correct Play

The wrong bettor should make a don't pass bet and then lay *single* odds against the point. Even though double odds will slightly reduce the house edge from 0.8% to 0.6%, a series of repeated points and the player's bankroll will quickly disappear.

Then the wrong bettor should make one, and if he's more aggressive, two don't come wagers, lay single odds against the come points, and stop.

Those are the only bets a wrong bettor should make.

To Summarize

Right Bettors:

Most Conservative:
1. Pass-line wager and full odds.
2. One come bet with full odds.

Conservative:
1. Pass-line wager and full odds.
2. Two come bets with full odds.

Aggressive:
1. Pass-line wager and full odds.
2. Two come bets and full odds.
3. Place bet on uncovered 6 or 8, or both.

If a come bet is repeated and won during the course of a roll, then make another come bet immediately. In other words, the most conservative bettor will have a come bet always working, that is, being bet or in action. The conservative bettor will have two come bets always working, as will the most aggressive player.

Wrong Bettors:

Most Conservative:
   1. Don't pass bet, laying single odds.

Conservative:
   1. Don't pass bet, laying single odds.
   2. One don't come bet, laying single odds.

Aggressive:
   1. Don't pass bet, laying single odds.
   2. One don't come bet, laying single odds.
   3. A second don't come bet, laying single odds.

XI. Money Management

Money management is an integral part of any successful gambling method. First of all, you should never play with money you can't afford to lose, or that would cause you financial or emotional discomfort if you lost it.

Gambling should be a fun thing, and exciting, but it can't be that if you're too emotionally involved. If that's the case, do something else, but don't gamble.

But, if you can handle the action, then divide your bankroll by fifty and that should be your unit for betting purposes. In other words, if you bring $50 to the table, don't bet more than $1 as your basic unit. With $100, this means $2 bets. Only if you have at least $250 should you be betting $5 at a time.

This is conservative, but will allow you to stay at a craps table for a long time, and may allow you to catch a hot roll, if you're a right player, or a long cold table, if you're betting wrong.

Try to double your money, and if you do that, quit. That's a good win in craps. If you can't do that, and you find you're winning $50 when you brought $100 to the table, and it's choppy, going nowhere, leave.

Another good time to leave is at the end of a hot roll, if you're a right bettor. Hot rolls don't come often.

Or, conversely, if you're betting wrong, and the dice are ice cold, with only craps and point numbers coming out on the come-out, and then 7s killing the point numbers time after time, leave when the dice start to turn, when 7s and 11s begin to show on the come-out and a point is repeated.

What if you're losing? Set a limit to your losses. The best way is to play with a bankroll you can afford to lose in that session of play. If you lose your one-session bankroll, leave the table. Above all, don't reach in for money after you've lost what you had in the rails.

The first loss is the cheapest. There'll be other games, other times. There'll always be time for more action at craps. Don't make the mistake of taking one terrible loss at one table. That's not the way smart gamblers handle losses.

Leave a winner if possible. A small win is better than any loss. You can't go wrong leaving a winner, remember that. Let's win!

XII. Glossary of Craps Terms

Any Craps—A one-roll wager that the next throw of the dice will come up 2, 3 or 12, craps numbers.

Any Seven—A one-roll wager that the next throw of the dice will come up a 7.

Back Line—Another term for the **Don't Pass** line.

Bar the 12 (or 2)—Making either number a standoff for wrong bettors, thus enabling the casino to keep its edge on don't pass and don't come bets.

Betting Right—Betting that the dice will win, by wagering on the pass-line and come.

Betting Wrong—Wagering that the dice won't win, or won't pass by betting on don't pass and don't come.

Big 6 and Big 8—An even-money wager that the 6 or 8, whichever is bet, will come up before a 7 is rolled.

Boxman—The casino employee who is in charge of an individual craps game. He is seated between the two dealers on base.

Buy the 4 and 10—Paying a 5% commission so the payoffs on these place numbers will be at 2-1.

Change Color—Changing casino chips into smaller or larger denominations.

Chips—Also known as **Casino Checks**—The tokens, usually of clay composition, that are used instead of cash by the players.

Come Bet—A wager made after the come-out roll, with the same rules as govern a pass-line bet.

Come-Out Roll—The roll that establishes a point for don't pass and pass-line bettors.

Craps—The term for the numbers 2, 3 and 12; which also gives the game its name.

Crap Out—The rolling of a 2, 3 or 12 on the come-out.

Crew—The dealers who staff the craps table.

Dealer—A uniformed employee of the casino who is either on base or a stickman at the craps table.

Dice—The cubes marked from 1 to 6 which, when rolled by a shooter, determine all wins and losses in the game of casino craps.

Die—The singular of dice.

Disk—Also known as **Buck, Marker Puck**—A white and black round object which shows whether there's a come-out roll coming up, or, if placed, shows the point number.

Don't Come Bet—A wager against the dice made after the come-out roll, subject to the same rules as a Don't Pass bet.

Don't Pass Bet—A wager prior to the come-out roll that the dice won't win, or pass.

Double Odds Bet—A free odds wager which is double the underlying bet.

Easy Way—The rolling of either 4, 6, 8 or 10 other than as a pair.

Edge—The advantage the house has on any wager. Also known as **Casino Advantage** or **Vigorish**.

Even-Money—A payoff at odds of 1-1.

Field Bet—A one-roll wager that the next number thrown will be a 2, 3, 4, 9, 10, 11 or 12.

Floorman—A casino executive who supervises one or more craps tables.

Free-Odds Bet—A wager made in addition to an underlying bet that is paid off at correct odds.

Front Line—Another term for **Pass-Line**.

Hardway Bet—A wager that the 4, 6, 8 or 10 will be rolled as a pair before they're rolled easy or a 7 is thrown.

Horn Bet—A one-roll wager combining the numbers 2, 3, 11 and 12.

Hot Roll—A long series of dice throws where the pass-line and right bettors win.

Lay Wager—Betting against a point number showing by paying a 5% commission.

Layout—The imprinted surface of a craps table, showing all the wagers that can be made, divided into separate areas.

Off—A term to signify that certain bets will not be at risk on the next roll of the dice.

On Base—The term for the dealers other than the stickman.

One-Roll Bets—Wagers determined by the next roll of the dice.

Pass—A winning decision for the right bettors.

Pass-Line Bet—A wager that the dice will win, or pass, made before the come-out roll.

Place Bets and Numbers—The wager that either one or more of the following numbers will come up before a 7 is rolled. The Place Numbers are 4, 5, 6, 8, 9 and 10.

Pit Boss—The casino executive in charge of all the craps tables comprising a craps pit.

Point, Point Numbers—The numbers 4, 5, 6, 8, 9 or 10 established on the come-out roll.

Press, Press A Bet—Increasing a winning bet, usually by doubling it.

Proposition Bet, Center Bet—Those wagers which are made in the center of the layout.

Rails—The grooved area on top of the table where players keep their chips.

Right Bettor—A bettor who wagers that the dice will pass, or win.

Seven-Out—The rolling of a 7 after a point has been established, losing the pass-line wager.

Shooter—The player who is rolling the dice.

Single-Odds Bet—A free odds wager equal to the underlying bet.

Stickman—The dealer who controls the dice and also calls the game.

Tip—A gratuity given to a dealer by a player. Also called a **Toke**.

Working—A term that the bets are at risk on the next roll of the dice.

Wrong Bettor—A player who wagers that the dice will lose by making Don't Pass and Don't Come bets.